THIS METAL

THIS METAL

Poems by

JOSEPH BATHANTI

Press 53
Winston-Salem

Press 53
PO Box 30314
Winston-Salem, NC 27130

First Edition

Cover design by Kevin Morgan Watson

Cover art © 1996 by Philip Delucia

Author photo by Jan Hensley

Printed on acid-free paper

ISBN 978-1-935708-28-5

for Joan, Jacob and Beckett

and in memory of my parents, Joseph D. and Roselyn Bathanti

Acknowledgments

Grateful acknowledgment is extended to the following journals in which some of these poems, in some cases different versions, first appeared; and, especially to Saint Andrews College Press, under whose imprint this volume originally appeared in 1996:

"Softball" and "Wrestling Practice, Sunday Morning, 1969" in *Aethlon: The Journal of Sport Literature*; "Wrestling Practice, Sunday Morning, 1969" in *Aethlon Sport Literature Anthology*; "Aunt Nina in Midair" in *America*; "From the Photograph of the Church Steps, September 3, 1947" in *The Asheville Review*; "October" in *Bay Leaves*; "I Will Mark the Tattler" in *California Quarterly*; "Washing Her Ruined Boy" in *The Chattahoochee Review*; "Grazziella" in *The Crescent Review*; "The Center Fielder" in *Crucible*; "Son of a Priest" in *Cumberland Poetry Review*; "Daria" and "1961" in *The Devil's Millhopper*; "Epistle to Sal" in *Dominion Review*; "Uncles" in *The Greensboro Review*; "Washing Her Ruined Boy" in *The Imaginative Spirit: Literary Heritage of Charlotte and Mecklenburg County, North Carolina*; "1961," "Daria," and "The Hollow" in *Independence Boulevard*; "The Headstone" in *Italian Americana*; "Softball" in *Line Drives: An Anthology of Contemporary Baseball Poems*; "Daria" in *Louisiana Literature*; "Sister" in *Lullwater Review*; "A Better Life" in *The Lyricist*; "Paolo Mio" in *Manhattan Poetry Review*; "Mendicant on a Bridge" in *Milkweed Chronicle*; "Let the Boy Try" in *The Nebraska Review*; "My Father Rising" in *Outer Banks Magazine*; "Daily Mass" and "My Sister's Childhood" in *The Panhandler*; "Courting the Chatham Girls," "Evening Late Summer" and "Turns" in *Pembroke Magazine*; "Mayday" in *The Pittsburgh Quarterly*; "Kyrie" in *Southern Humanities Review*; "October" in *South Dakota Review*; "The Death of East Liberty" and "Paolo Mio" in *Town Creek Poetry*; "Washing Her Ruined Boy" in *Thunder and Honey*; Paolo Mio in *VIA: Voices in Italian Americana*; "The Death of East Liberty" in *West Branch*; "Forbes Field" in *The Worcester Review*.

The following poems also appeared in the chapbook, *Communion Partners,* published in 1986 by Briarpatch Press: "The Center Fielder," "Communion Partners," "Larimer Avenue," "Mendicant on a Bridge," "Paolo Mio," "A Player Without A Game," "Three Rivers," and "Sempre Fidele" (as "Semper Fidelis").

Cover icon: Philip Delucia

Contents

III. This Metal

Introduction

by Mary Jo Bona

When an avid reader of contemporary poetry discovers a book so full of warmth and eloquent exactitude, she is grateful and excited to read more by the author. This was my first experience of reading Joseph Bathanti's fourth book of poems, *This Metal.* I felt humbled by reading a poet whose voice was strong, but I was simultaneously dazzled by a vocabulary rich in metaphor and inflected by the language of faith and place. In preparation for penning this introduction, I reread *This Metal* and experienced again Bathanti's linguistic precision which creates a physical world both wounding and supportive of the people within. Winner of the 1997 Oscar Arnold Young Award for the best book of poems by a North Carolina writer, *This Metal* is Joseph Bathanti's homage to the world of his ancestors, his Catholic boyhood, and his inevitable exodus out of the old neighborhood of East Liberty—an Italian enclave—in adulthood.

Perhaps the mother's monologue in the poem, "Washing her Ruined Boy," summarizes the elegiac tone of Bathanti's book: "what he's assailed by is loss, / . . . Already he's bent on making / this mourning his life." Reconciling inevitable loss is the function of the poet, and for Joseph Bathanti, his *felix culpa.* For in these pages, Bathanti recounts several losses to which he bears witness: his Italian American forbears; the closing of the Pittsburgh steel mills; and the formative years of a pre-Vatican II Catholic upbringing. Comprised of three sections—*Prometheus, Son of a Priest,* and *This Metal*—Bathanti's poetry focuses throughout on topics of family, work, place, and religion. For those raised Catholic and sent to parochial schools, reading such poems as "My Sister's Childhood," and "Wrestling Practice," can still induce shivers. I will respond to Bathanti's use of the language of Catholicism within the paragraphs below.

Bathanti intersperses his poignant poems of Italian heritage with regular ruminations on what was by mid-century the great American pastime: baseball. Poems such as "Forbes Field," and

"The Babe Ruth Story," interpenetrate with the landscape of Pittsburgh itself, as the speaker smells coal coming from the river and sees "the sky . . . parched / by stack-fire and a thousand boom crane spindles" ("Forbes Field"). For a boy like Joseph, baseball gave him imaginative license to be a champion, a position of triumph for which he prayed fervently and which granted him mental latitude, or, as he writes in "The Center Fielder," "sudden deliverance . . . homage to an illusory self." No such physically exalting alternative existed for his sister, Marie, "a virtuous, myopic girl; /gifted, mysterious," who was made to suffer in silence as her brother was beaten by a nun; Bathanti refers to his sister's "small hands petalled across her face— / nowhere else for my eyes" ("My Sister's Childhood").

The ordinary harshness of everyday life is evinced in *This Metal*, especially in those poems detailing the lives of working-class men. Such poems recall the work of his father and neighborhood men, those mill workers who also suffer silently from accidents, steel strikes, and ill health. In the aptly titled "Prometheus," Bathanti recalls the Greek myth in order to honor his father, who was chained to his own rock for forty years at the Edgar Thomson Works, the first mill Andrew Carnegie opened in America. The hero in this poem is not the millionaire industrialist, but rather and of course Bathanti's industrious father who suffers and survives an arm injury 'and hoists into the still night sky / his flaming hand,' returning after the accident, titan-like, to the mill. During one of the several strikes that required his father to find other work, the third-grader Bathanti recalls his father's popularity at their Catholic church, as his janitorial job gave him the "keys to every sacramental door." Recalling that time allows the poet to associate his father with the sacred as he cleans the tabernacle and the sacristy cabinets; Joseph touches "Every sacred object" made special by his father's care ("Son of a Priest"). Often in literature, we read representations of, if not tortured, then at least difficult father-son relations; what a happy reprieve to read of a father-son relationship not marred by anger, violence, or absence. As Joseph wrote to me in a recent email message, his father was "quiet and shy and modest—but constant and kind and gentle." These poems bear eloquent and sustained witness to that relationship and it is beautiful to see. Joseph's comment to me is brought to fruition in his titular poem, "This Metal," in which the poet writes in tribute to his father: "He has held on all his life / not talking."

Bathanti's necessary decision to break the silence of his male ancestors aligns him with such poets as Maria Mazziotti Gillan, Sharon Olds, and Edward Hirsch, whose poetic task has been to record in unflinching detail the difficult lives of family members. Bathanti's ancestral past compels him to consider how the immigrant experience permanently estranged the males in his family, who bequeathed to their children the complicated gift of silence. The poet endows his grandfather with the gift of fluency, as Paolo grieves for the loss of his Italian homeland and suffers dislocation in the new world: "God did not prepare me for this bitch country. / My hand is against it. / Let my blood make peace" ("A Better Life"). Dedicated to "Paolo Battiante, 1874-1968," "A Better Life" orthographically gives the grandfather back his name, which was changed in spelling after emigration; that Joseph Bathanti writes the poem as a monologue equally allows the grandfather's voice to find utterance in the new tongue. The poem thus functions as both a gesture of redemption and *rispetto* (respect).

That Bathanti gives voice to these silent men is testimonial to his desire to legitimate the personal histories of his family. Incorporating images of fire and metal to commemorate the work of his fathers, Bathanti mythologizes his grandfather's American experience by comparing him to the god of fire, "raving / as Prometheus, stripped of fire and forge" ("Sempre Fidele"). In keeping with the Italian American tendency to merge the sacred and the secular, the Christian and the primordial, Bathanti embraces the contradictory nature of his family's heritage and his life as a Catholic school boy. Contrasting elements cohere vividly in Bathanti's verse. Of his grandfather, the poet writes, "But after he drunk, / we could all hear him: rasping / his *compline* in dialect ... invoking Jesu / and Garibaldi in one breath" ("Paolo Mio"). Bathanti describes his elementary school teacher,

Sister Daria, as "croaking out *The Sanctus* / as she finished us with sucker punches" ("Daria"). Both poems are, in effect, hymns of praise for his grandfather's strength in the face of loss and his teacher's courage during a school fire in which she saved the children and sacrificed herself.

But it is perhaps my re-reading of the poem "Wrestling Practice" that truly struck me like Sister Daria's sucker punch of yore. It packs a wallop in several ways: indeed, this poem about childhood wrestling is the longest in this book and its gravitas is both literal and metaphorical. Joseph reiterated to me in a recent email exchange that he was inculcated and indoctrinated in his Catholic boyhood and that playing sports was a way for him to achieve spirituality through immolation, mortifying the flesh to achieve purity of spirit. This explanation, recalling medieval sensibilities, certainly explained to me—a parochial Catholic school girl who did not participate in any sport—the ways in which boys could exert their physicality in socially sanctioned ways—through beating their classmates, achieving "good boy" status by hating their opponents: "fifty Catholic bodies at war." Despite hating wrestling, the young Joseph inchoately recognizes that this sport is one way to survive the kind of repression required by Catholicism and to demonstrate paradoxically through the staunch requirement of wrestling a "narrative of effacement" to "make weight."

Playing sports has often been conflated with spirituality and becoming less of oneself to attain more is wrestling's goal and certainly the goal of Brother Coach whose "three hundred pounds / of concupiscence" is not lost on the boy wrestlers. Desire repressed turns boys into warriors, "hunger artists / have stretched them into haters," and the poet's "sacred occasion" occurs when he weighs in privately, "stripped of every pretense, / but survival." The boy "[mounts]" the scale, but he only allows himself to think that this action is similar to how he might "kiss / a girl." Wrestling practice is not without its eroticism intensified by Latin commands and Catholic liturgy. "Wrestling Practice" comprises many of the finest elements in Bathanti's book of poetry, offering a finely honed slice of Catholic school inflected by American sports, and the ways in which boys are socialized to negotiate their masculinity at a young age.

Another finely honed slice of life surrounding many of the poems in *This Metal* is the Pittsburgh of mid-century and beyond, with its steel mills, fires, smoke, and dirt. In "The Death of East Liberty," Bathanti memorializes the place of his youth in his recounting of his losses resulting from urban renewal: "Half the voters could not speak English / to save their homes. . . . The men sat in rubble / and wept with the jack hammers." Such lines deserve to be read alongside Felix Stefanile's "The Bocce Court on Lewis Avenue" (*The Dance at St. Gabriel's*), Tina De Rosa's *Paper Fish*, and Sandra Gilbert's "Empty Nest" (*Blood Pressure*), for they each illuminate the intimacy between place and identity, between power and poverty. I remember the line in the Epilogue of Tina De Rosa's poetic novel, *Paper Fish*, in which the author writes, "The city said the Italian ghetto should go, and before the people could drop their forks and say, pardon me? the streets were cleared" (120). Such is the case for Joseph Bathanti's East Liberty, an Italian enclave that undergoes what was conveniently called "urban renewal," and the poet's response to this loss is as intense and sorrowful as the other writers in the canon of Italian America: "The wrecking ball emptied the sky like an atom bomb." The community experiences "death," and, despite their impoverished origins and lack of political power, this was their neighborhood, their community, imagined and lived.

"Three Rivers," another place poem, pays tribute to Pittsburgh's "congress of rivers," as Bathanti melds sacred and secular in his invocatory memory of place: "like those rivers, / there was the illusion of triune destiny, / water enough to buoy three lifetimes. / We would never part. / Their fathoms willed us to aim at fire, / thread ourselves into a birthright ringed / with steel and lonely men fishing." Despite the poet's self-reflexive scolding—"I'm sick of recounting this past"—in his important poem "Suicide: Running Across the Meadow Street Bridge, Thanksgiving Day, 1993," Bathanti recalls many of the themes of his poetry in order to be "exorcised / of the old neighborhood that bars my entry / into a new trope." Bathanti's freedom to make his "taboo run" through his old neighborhood now dogged by gangs and guns has as much to do with his gender and his drive to understand the inexorable connection between ancestry and American identity, between Italians and blacks, between homeless and sheltered, between poet and suicide victim. The poet sees a young black man fit high-top gym shoes on a homeless junky before jumping over the bridge to his death. In this act, the poet realizes that gestures of redemption are awe-inspiring and silent. Struggling with his faith, Bathanti invokes the aid of Christ to ask of Italians and blacks "grizzling / in their cerements . . . how / of his liturgy they made this dying place." As in other books—*Communion Partners*, *Anson County*, *Feast of All Saints*, *Land of Amnesia*, and his most recent, *Restoring Sacred Art*, Bathanti remembers the falling, silent ones of our shared past, believing that poetry acts as a quiet and forceful redemption.

The reprinting of *This Metal* illustrates another kind of redemption in an age of two-second bites and one-hundred forty character tweets. A reissued book of poetry reflecting the range and depth of Joseph Bathanti's skill sends a more mindful message to those of us who read and teach and talk endlessly about poetry: we go to poetry to understand and more fully inhabit our lives, learning to live more peacefully with others whose lives are different but no less vital than ours.

Mary Jo Bona
January 2012
Stony Brook University

I. PROMETHEUS

Paolo Mio

Carrying a smith's tools
in a land which would not brook his fire,
he planted seeds,
and each year the birds

took his first fruit, leaving him
to rave woodenly like a false prophet,
one eye blind,
the other like a smoked marble.

When his wife died, he buried her
out of country in a hill
filled with Lutherans
and never returned.

Hiding in the grape arbor,
I felt his anger coursing through me.
Even then I knew
I was his Hercules.

One eye squinted, I can see
his now-boxed body alive
in the shuttered room
where he slept alone

and danced the Tarantella
in Sunday shirt and gold watch,
brooded over Chianti and fierce Parodis.
His daughters, whom he could not distinguish

from fishwives, pulled me from the door.
But after he was drunk,
we all heard him: rasping
his *compline* in dialect, roaring

with the blasted mouth of a soldier,
invoking *Jesu*
and Garibaldi in one breath.
There are relics of him strewn

throughout the garden:
watch chain, cigar stubs,
shards of shattered bottles,
a broken spade.

His shirt flaps in the wind.
The scarecrow wears his fedora.
I lift my hands to bless the birds
that swoop down on these elegies.

Sempre Fidele

Proper of the Season

It is not true
the red pepper is hottest,
but the slender green,
its flame a drug for the spleen.
The old man eats one after another
with Roman elan.
Brine-sopped Lupi beans;
eggplant and Locatelli,
sharp enough to bloody a cat's mouth;
wine olives, fennel, *baccala*;
calamari; smelts,
bone and gristle;
versicle and prayer,
whiskey-coaxed.
Eighty-seven years of fire in his mouth,
anger left for dirt.

Litany

For a moment he is supplicant,
memory his hair shirt.
He recalls the smell of olive blossoms
spreading the hills of Foggia.
He does not wish to die in this hemisphere,
but where the land reckons his death warble.
A man who leaves his country
is forever whelped by illusion,
never knowing whenness from destiny.
Then it is the old fire

he must thresh. Anathema
prevails upon the spurious tongue
of whiskey, throngs the room
like burning ancestors,
drinks vendetta.

Midnight

It is his quiet son, my good father,
who must put him to bed raving
as Prometheus, stripped of fire and forge,
raved at each pass of the eagle.
The women beg him to make Easter Duty.
Shrovetide approaches.
He smokes in bed, blasphemes.
The parish priest is a *gavone*,
un porco who eats too much.
One of his daughters is dying,
but he doesn't realize.
In *Italia*, he would have been a baron;
and I, the apple of his only eye,
would cross the Apennines
to the Mediterranean.

Sunday

Dawn, he sweetens his coffee
with Anisette. Then to the garden:
exhumes the fig trees;
slashes the fox grape;
plants rows of parsley, *basilico*,
garlic, onion, oregano.
I wake.

Hoarfrost cracks on my window.
I scrape into its welts my name.
Crows circle the orchard.
Thunderheads well.
I find my grandfather in his shed,
smoking Parodis, singing
the same two lines of a *canzonetta*.
Early mass bells split the black clouds, ringing.
Earth turns its brown graves to the sun,
the forgotten woman in the wrong hill.
Playing between his black shoes,
I watch that bad eye of his,
some vision silvered beneath,
a mirror possessed
by its own whelmed image.

Lullaby

Through the night, praying for snow,
I have nightmares in which I'm dead drunk,
but incorruptible. Women
touch me and answer my questions.
I wake to snow,
sure my novena conjured it.
All day, flakes big as half-dollars
softening the world's angles.
I don't want to play, but be alone.
As I burrow into the white meninx,
there is a crossing over.
My blood knots. A strange fealty
for this element adjures me to sleep.
They call; but I am drifted over,
outside them, sovereign.

Memento Mori

I sit between my father and sister,
knees pressed to our '56 Plymouth's heater.
Gumto's Greenhouse is warm,
but its sad smell of flowers turns my stomach.
Marie can name each genus.
To us, it is a game:
our Lenten office at Saint Peter's,
helping our father find
his mother's moiety of feudal dirt;
her cantle of America, here in this cemetery
by mistake, alone among Lutherans;
choked by catbrier and morning glory.
We trudge uphill behind him.
I fit my boot into each print he makes.
Each year the plot eludes us,
the trove of bones I imagine loves me.
The old cross keens, half the name—
Battiante—obscured.
My father saws the furring strips,
taps in the nails for me to pound. Marie
letters upon the new cross the name
of her namesake: *Maria Christina.*
Seedlings rooted and watered,
my father does not make us pray.
From a squat at the steep
grave-head, he holds us.
We've inherited this land,
his father's venial blunder, leering
blasted from the opaque cornea.
We can see the Allegheny
pushing west toward the equinox,
its surrounding slopes still mauled by snow.

Back down the hill, we find
a dead pheasant and bury it too.
Left here I would never find my way home,
wandering, forever a child,
in this odd quarry of unfamiliar ghosts.
I placate stone in a blaze
of *Hail Mary's* and *Glory Be's*—
already sorry for everything.

The Feast of The Assumption, 1920

The Papists are at their sorcery in the streets.
Acolytes carry Our Lady's blue banner
tacked with dollar bills,
censers seething myrrh and frankincense.
The band plays.
Immigrants sing from the stoops:
Ave Maria, Regina Coeli.
Above them, in a small room,
a woman is dead to childbirth.
A boy too young to confess
watches his mother lifted
from the cooling board and carried
into the dancing streets.
He expects the earth to shudder.
It does not, but his mother levitates
above the gray-gloved bearers.

Nunc Dimittis

Running from my grandfather's garden,
I catch in a skein of grape vine
and crash through the lintel of my world
into the cherry orchard. Humming *O Bambino*,
he comes upon me, shrieks,
Jesu Christe; then crabs off, hailing
in his matrix of English my father
who comes galloping.
The old man waits for him to lift me.
For a moment it's as though they pray
over me. Together
they gently pick the pits and spalls
of fruit from my face. My blood
thuds to earth, a pittance
of shrift the earth accepts
beyond provenance and ancestry—
our blood-leaf.

PHYSIC

No way of knowing when the door would open,
my father's shoes staring up at me,
and it would be my turn.
I never tried to run, but took instead

his sorrowful hand. He led me
down the hall, past the bathroom,
three stairs up, in an alcove,
where my sister, naked

in her sweating pixie, sat
catatonic on the toilet, letting spill
out of her the caustic silt.
Seeing her stripped even of shame,

hurting, in horror at her body, so like mine,
smelling the carbolated vasoline, spying
laid out on my parents' bed the bleeding
hot water bottle, nozzles, tubes, hoses,

their open arms and placating smiles—
that's when I panicked
and lashed myself to the banister.
My father prized me from its balusters.

As my clothes were removed,
I heard as though through an amnion
promises—chocolate pudding,
a new baseball bat—endearments,

their need for me to be brave
so they could endure it, my mouth,
as I was pierced, filling
with our best towels' pile,

my mother calling me, *Pigeon,*
her voice a bit frantic, unsure why
they were doing this, my father
clucking tenderly, *Hold still, Buddy,*

we're almost done, his hands like manacles.
Then the fever streamed into me,
and I closed my eyes and drowned.
I had no more fight.

It had happened. Blameless,
they had done it to me.
As I struggled to keep still
so the hell that had me pinned

to the bed in which I was engendered
would not detonate,
I, in my own ignorance, absolved them
because my catechism had taught

that this is what it might be like:
life somehow obtained through death;
that all along it had been love, salvation
laved scalding, unbearable into me.

The Center Fielder

As a little boy, dreaming
of your first fly ball, you courted
the edge of your earth, unmindful
of the wall which measured risk.

You realized early that, by running,
you could touch anything, coveting
each ball's flight, taunting the wall.
There's no way of knowing when a child

will take to a ball. As you grew older,
there was nothing you wouldn't do for it;
though you remained humble,
often abandoning your perch at the warning

track to kneel and dig the ball from the earth.
Watching you throw was like being moved
by the wind. The first time you dove,
people were bedeviled,

skeptical of such sudden deliverance.
Your flight seemed homage to an illusory self,
so insanely heroic were the catches you made,
defying the wall against all elements.

Batters grew superstitious, crossing
themselves, rearranging their feet and hands—
foolhardy to hit it toward you.
But there were always the Philistine

sluggers who charted the length
of destiny beyond your clutch.
You became the object of their scorn.
They tested you with their power:

the ball's ascent leaves you transfixed.
A quick pirouette,
then you are all speed and fixity
(and now it occurs to me that,

each time, you were dreaming),
a look of utter astonishment
upon your uplifted face
as if you'd just witnessed

body and soul reeved in mid-air.
For that union you soar, outstretched
hand, eyes opaque, knowing
when you fall to earth,

you will find the ball in your glove.
Somehow you have gleaned the secret
of catching; but you will not look
at us surrounding you—

only the earth
and sky of your generous dream,
deep in center,
dead against the wall.

LARIMER AVENUE

It's a mile drive, twelve city blocks—down
Highland, then left at Saint Marie

where houses squat in rows and brick
layers and cement finishers, grayed

with mortar, slump home to supper. Kids
play Indian-ball in the schoolyard.

The first bottles unsheath on Chookie's corner.
Old men think on porch gliders. They know

where we're going: across Meadow Street
Bridge into the gut of ancestry—Larimer

Avenue, where every John thinks he's a gangster.
Tinhorn politicians—snap-brim Stetsons, menacing

suits—slouch in Genevieve's doorway.
In their shadow, children apprentice,

dodging cars, pitching pennies and craps
in corner joint lees. Crusty

merchants close shop, harangue one another
in Calabrese and Piedmontese. Old man

Labriola sidles warily onto the sidewalk,
checks his flanks as if expecting ambush,

covers the olive barrels, suspiciously
lugs hanging tuns of provolone and salami

back into his musty store. Ash Wednesday:
Alfred DiStefano, eating his last

Sicilian olives from Labby's barrels,
took six neat ones in the belly from a phantom

Caddy—right there on the cement
in a suite of blood and olive oil.

The four of us sit in familiar quadrants
of our '63 Bel Air. Long black

and Latin faces stare plaintively from each
window: in the garrets above Paradise

and Costa; in Stoebner Alley, trashed
with old soldiers—Manischevitts, Wild

Irish Rose. On across Larimer Bridge—
Rimini's Bakery sweetening the air—

over which Charles Harris, chased
by Chester's German Shepherds after

he robbed the station, hurled himself
to escape—and only broke a leg.

1959

I'm commanded to march
to the lavatory stall where I'll be "settled
once and for all." There I smell
butts stuck to the urinal wall,
the disinfectant puck's perfume
rising off her habit as she goes to work.

The autumn of 1959 flays me
in its final throes of repression:
This is for Ike

                      and

This is for Joe

                      and

This is for Ozzie and Harriet,
The Good Shepherd,
Our boys in Korea.
This is only a test.

My eyes find the phone number
I can call for a "decent blowjob"
(not knowing what one is)
and "Eat me" stabbed into the toilet seat.
The bowl water reflects the image
of my first nun behind me,
like the exquisite Saint Bridgette—
thirty-six inches and her triune of vows.
I'm all she has and I'll not cry.
The only thing I really know
is how to hold it in.

The schoolyard's four storey smokestack
incinerates first grade readers: Dick
and Jane, Puff, Spot, Mother and Father.
Ashes. In Rome, John launches
Vatican II. Kennedy slouches
toward the Potomac. Across
from the schoolhouse, angels
the sisters call Negroes suck Tokay
poorboys. A mutt-scuttled bitch dances
on six legs in the middle of Flavel Street.

When I am done getting it,
she locks me in the office
with the school's only phone.
I dial Emerson 1-8104—
my mother laid off at home
scrubbing the basement floor—
and I get the busy signal.

As for the Jew,
he is dying
to escape His kingdom of air.
Like all hard-luck felons,
He can't connect His cross
with what He did to get it.
I climb the principal's desk,
from the wall lift and turn Him
upside-down like a sword
and wait for His wife
in her black get-up.

THE BABE RUTH STORY

The last rites of the Catholic Church were administered on July 21, but Ruth rallied again after that. He left the hospital on the evening of July 26 to attend the premier of The Babe Ruth Story. He was very uncomfortable watching the film and left before it was over.

— Robert W. Creamer, *The Babe*

A hand-fed sixteen
millimeter sprayed black
and white the school cellar wall,
a nun caressing a flashlight
on the periphery of the dust-flecked film beam.

I kept at home above my bed
a poster of the real Babe Ruth.
Pinstriped, throned, with his
Yankee crown and the enormous
bat thrown slant like a scepter
at his shoulder, he looked nothing
like William Bendix, who played the Babe
like *The Life of Reilly*—
a dear sheepish lug who with
four pounds of ashe and horsehide
dreamt himself,
then gave his life away.

Crouched in my metal chair
beneath the soft Cathode ray,
feeling on my lips the breast-
like give of the marshmallows I ate,
and on my tongue their cloying,
I was happy.
Only a good beating could make me cry.

THE HEADSTONE

My father has never talked much.
His father, dead today, after ninety-four years,
was the same. Tucked in the barber's chair,
I can't remember a single sentence passed between them.

Fred jacks me up and spins me, grumbling
to keep still or I'll be using my ear for an ashtray.
He tells dirty jokes and kids me about girls.
He calls them "broads."

Through the mirror he winks at my father,
lounging on the shine stand,
not appearing to pay attention.
"Didn't your old man run a shop

down on Mayflower?" Fred asks.
My father does not say yes, does not say no.
"He was a real sport. Wasn't he?"
I wonder why he doesn't correct this barber.

Yet I feel the pall of silence stealing over me.
My grandfather refused to speak English.
We knew when he lifted his hand,
he was finished. He would drink wine

and no longer look at anyone.
I don't know what went on
between him and my father.
Fred's razor rivets my mirrored stare,

reflecting a dismissed Peabody shift
strolling toward Vento's Pizza.
My father replaces me in the chair
as I wander into the back

where Frankie, the Shine, plops
on a stack of *Playboys*, writing numbers.
I'm tempted to lay a buck
on my grandfather's birth date.

All those years, shrouded
in that big chrome and porcelain chair,
I've listened to bookies swear
on their sainted mothers

that a number played on a corpse is sure to hit.
My father sits in the chair
in the window, sunlight streaming
down the slopes of the white sheet,

his clipped hair black against it.
I haven't wanted to ask him if Papa had a priest.
On the way home, we stop for hotdogs
at The Original. Moe, the owner, mentions

to my dad: "Sorry about your old man,"
then nods, "Is that your kid?"
Our last stop is to see about the stone.
Pofi sits in his yard among the markers,

sun glittering in the silver aggregate.
It was his father's business.
He still uses the tools the old man brought over from Naples.
He gets up to shake hands with my father.

"This is a hell of a thing," he says.
"What do you want on it?" When after a while
my father doesn't answer, he looks at me
and asks, "What do you want on it?"

A BETTER LIFE

— *Paolo Battiante*
(1874-1968)

Now a thousand kilometers from Apulia,
the sea is an oracle
coiling at the gunwales:

I will have a son who will not love water.
His name will be taken.
No matter.

I will remain unknown.
Where I live unacquainted,
even with the ghosts who needle me,

it is dark without the sight
of the eye plucked by pigiron
on my last ride with Garibaldi.

Its final glimpse—
my stallion on fire, a scarecrow
wrapped in the Padrone's red blouse,

Maria holding a red apple—
yet swills in a trench
along the Gulf of Taranto.

Do not suppose my grief, nor language.
What love remains is planted.
A seed dropped in my spit prospers.

I sail to America with trowel
and hammer, one eye, no voice.
To my children I bequeath silence—

what they will loathe in me,
and have to break alone like the wedge
of this stone sea in themselves.

God did not prepare me for this bitch country.
My hand is against it.
Let my blood make peace.

GRAZZIELLA

Her grave silent scrutiny
of the huckster's vegetables

made me wary,
lest I speck her evil eye

and be roasted like peppers.
When she appeared, hair netted

like a black carapace, soothsaying,
penance-hawking,

our games fell to her mourning.
Hard black shoes soldiering

one after another each day
to church bells, bartering

with the sacraments for the soul of her lost
Napolitano; at Mount Carmel, scrabbling

through grave dirt, mumbling
antiphonies beneath a blue sky,

hunched over the tomb, hands
strapped with rosaries, crumbling

each indifferent clod, searching
for her lover's fist, upsetting

the geraniums, giving utterance
to each stone, impaling

me on the spine
of my own mortality.

WASHING HER RUINED BOY

That he would not cry this way
in front of his father
is no measure of greater love.
He simply apportions me what is mine.
As I run his bath
I watch him through the mirror,
YANKS piped gravely across his chest
in maroon block, as he undresses.
He's smooth and pretty
as his sister, but unlike her
he covets fame's witness.
I can hardly lift him
over the lip of the tub
where his regatta lists,
dry-docked and forgotten.
Tonight he does not buck my cleansing hand,
but leans into it, crying, as I bathe him—
still not sure that what he's assailed by is loss,
for what is there to lose in seven years?
Already he's bent on making
this mourning his life.
Each night he prays to be a champion.
I yearn to tell him he is right
to despair as I towel and wrap him,
languid, weeping, across my knees, wondering
if tonight he'll cry out in sleep as he kicks
that same elusive grounder through his dreams.
The one he's told me over and over—
incredulous that something bad could happen—
that had all the world to choose,
yet chose the earth he stood on
to pluck off and ruin him.

DAILY MASS

We knew that side door
at Saints Peter and Paul existed
to break the spirit of late comers—
that door of English yew
hewn by the flaming sword
of some sanctimonious angel
who had it in for school kids.
Oh, how my sister and I
leaned into it after running the last block
on those white mornings; then barged
into a rectitude of stained glass
like refugees crashing a cotillion,
snow snarling around us;
the thud of the vaulted door
announcing us red-handed
among the granite pillars.
We tore off our hats and mittens,
probed the Holy Water,
blessed our faces and coats—
nothing but the Consecration
between us and our reckoning Host.

MY SISTER'S CHILDHOOD

There exist no accounts
of trouble in my sister's childhood.
She was a virtuous, myopic girl;
gifted, mysterious, one to hesitate
with the secret word in the wee of night
when I tapped the wall that separated
our bedrooms and asked, "What is naked?"
And, though not quite happy about it,
she would know. When the nuns dragged me
to her classroom and beat me in front of her,
they forced her to stand
amidst her seated class. Akimbo
cross a chair I could make out
the pale blue veins
of the hand she placed on her desktop
to steady herself as she watched.
Even as the black board fell
I thought only of her rescue.
When finally I uncrooked myself,
I was required to turn and say,
"Thank you, Sister," to the gleaming
face that was not my sister's.
Then I looked at Marie,
her small hands petaled across her face—
nowhere else for my eyes.

EVENING LATE SUMMER

My dad blows smoke out
the Plymouth's window
as my mother walks smartly
across Meadow Street to Febraro's
where a tailor she sewed for is laid out.
We watch until she disappears,
a black sleeve snaking from within
to hold open the door.
Too young—thank God,
thank the brace of Saint Christophers
lanced to the sun-visor,
the magnetized Sacred Heart
at attention on the steel dashboard,
right arm raised like a traffic cop's—
to reckon the currency of dead tailors,
we listen to baseball on the radio
and puzzle over Pirate broadcaster,
Bob Prince's metaphors.
"We need a bloop and a blast," he says.
When Ducky Schofield chips
a Texas Leaguer into left,
he shouts, "That ball had eyes."
And when Gino Cimoli
parks a ninth inning pinch homer
into the streets of Pittsburgh
to win, two down, do or die,
he croons, "You can kiss it goodbye."
When my mother reappears,
Marie and I study her, then ask,
"What did he look like?"

"Like he was sleeping," she answers,
then hands us the memorial holy cards
I shuffle and cache
like a stack of all-stars.
Then to the Dairy Queen
at Silver Lake, and a spin
through Highland Park,
my sister and I narcotized
by shadows tumbling over the back seat,
the yellow eyes of kudu
and wildebeest blazing
from the zoo's roadside pens.

LINCOLN AVENUE

From our Lincoln duplex, crosscut
by black mortuaries and African temples,
I watched spectacular wakes.

Forbidden across the street, forbidden
around the corner, I mapped
my allotment of concrete, studying

walls sprayed with *fuck* and *nigger*,
against which nurses and stonecutters
died as they waited

for the last car up cemetery hill.
I had given up on my fairy godmother
and powdered my milk-teeth on the tracks.

Steel wheels on steel rails rutted
in gray ten pound cobbles screeched
and sparked. Streetcars

freighted straphangers to rib joints
and storefront clubs on the hill
where Joe Westray built The Ebony Lounge

next to The Church of Corpus Christi.
Sipping Iron City ponies,
guys with processes sat

on the street in folding chairs
eyeing our heap
as it lumbered us home.

Bedded while still light, I prayed
to sleep before nightmare,
certain I heard gunfire upstairs

from the ex-cop sleeping off speakeasy
whiskey, his sister screaming
"those black thugs" had poisoned his booze.

The night his heart exploded,
a paddy wagon fetched him, splashing
my room with its bloody siren.

I Cannot Look Away

On Aunt Jay's front porch sifting
through a Quinlan's Pretzel can filled
with the effects of her three sons, grown
and gone hipstering to California.
She's given me this to take my mind off things.
My mother is with my father at the hospital.
He's had his arm sliced nearly off.
My aunt has shown me where I'll sleep—
in the room with three beds and ship's wheel
lamp I may leave on all night.
She asks me what I saw.

Inside the can are rosaries;
beer bottle caps; scapulars; Scripto
lighter; Miraculous Medal; Jimmy
Piersall's autobiography, *Fear Strikes Out*;
a statue of Our Lady of Guadalupe;
pocket flashlight; magnifying
glass; a gorgeous knife, gilt
inlaid legend, *Como, Italia*;
screwdriver; and playing cards.
I slip the knife into my pocket,
flick open the silver lighter
and thumb the flywheel over flint
as I've seen my father do hundreds
of times before lighting up.
The flame coughs and lolls on its pilot.
When I snap it shut, there's the smell
of Butane. The lighter, as I squeeze
it in my palm, is warm.

I rifle through the cards.
Fifty-two women, flouting mortality,
float out and smile. Naked
women: with dogs, bottles, candles;
with other women; balancing
on their snowy perfect breasts
glasses of champagne.
Knowing what has happened
to my father, they gaze at me,
hysteria dripping from their eyes.
On the black and white tiles
of their bodies, impastoed
with my bloody longing
are his red footprints.

PROMETHEUS

When finally the cast comes off,
in place of my father's arm is a stranger's:
blackened indigo, inscribed
wrist to elbow, hairless,

with a long hyphenated catgut sentence
I'm unable to read. With his good arm,
he arranges it, its peculiar density,
like a deeply sleeping baby

one tries to bed without waking.
Even after the stitches come out,
the arm just lies there, denouncing
my father, its cocoa-buttered

incision threatening to open any moment
and push out its mangled red wires,
accidentally stripped by an ellipsoid
of jack-knifed aluminum.

Its empty icy hand has no feeling.
To test its strength, he squeezes
my hand, then simply smiles
without his might and drops it.

In his robe, nights, alone, smoking,
sipping red wine, trying to decant
the smashed goblets of blood lost,
the book he has no interest in laid aside,

he talks to the hand, opening
and closing around a rubber ball,
in a voice I've never heard.
He holds to it his cigarette.

Smoke rises to my hiding place on the landing.
His first swing back at the Basic Oxygen Plant,
the reneged hand, gloved, brushes a coke forge
and ignites. He feels nothing.

In his asbestos tunic, he goes on ladling
heat until another millwright cries out.
My father lifts his mask and stares
at his fingers guttering fire—

so favoring dream he smiles upon
the slag-gang slapping at him
and hoists into the steel night sky
his flaming hand.

II. SON OF A PRIEST

Son of a Priest

The year I was in third grade,
my father, who bided steel
strikes by odd-jobbing,

janitored at Saints Peter and Paul.
No nun dared strike me
with him in the building.

They loved him the way they loved
priests—a man with the run of things,
keys to every sacramental door.

He drove the snowplow and drank
with the Pastor. On Shrove
Tuesday, he placed over the Communion

of Saints the purple rags
of abnegation; then snatched them
off forty days later in the little hours

of Christ's comeback. He cleansed
the secret places; and I,
like the son of a priest, went with him

to reckon the holy fortress.
I put my face to the tabernacle,
squeezed behind the golden altar

(distraught it was made of wood),
rummaged the sacristy cabinets:
chalice, vestments, thurible, cruets.

At Our Lady's altar, I lit each votive
and kissed her feet.
Every sacred object, I touched.

I washed my face in holy water.
I drank it, mounted the pulpit.
With the confessor's stole around my neck,

I sat in his forgiving chair—
where I got scared, and went looking
for my father, swabbing the sanctuary

or high on a ladder, dusting
the mammoth Crucifix. Relieved,
I'd slink into Saint Joseph's Chapel,

where I was baptized,
and fall asleep
on its single red-cushioned pew.

Examining My Conscience

Back my eyes roll
back into the black sockets of time,

picturing my soul a vaporous androgynous shade
muscling around my insides,

growing more and more dyspeptic
as I unwittingly pock it.

Its crazed brother, conscience,
a fogbound yellow, welters it out with him.

The unacquainted Siamese twins,
drunk in the counting house, squabbling

over venial and mortal. I must confess
and everything's on edge—

something to be over with
like shot or enema, then cookies.

I cross the confessional's carven threshold.
Inside the catnapping Jesuit pouts.

"Bless me, Father, for I have sinned."
The grate slides by, leaving

but a hatch of black gauze between our chins.
In my head the rickety machinery begins.

The psyche is a cellar pointed with bone.
God is dead is this summer's song.

Jesus Christ had a girlfriend.
My mind needs punched.

Even as I confess to lying I lie, fearing
to confide that I've robbed the sacristy

of sacred wine, the Record Mart of 45's:
The Temptations and Jagger's "Paint It Black."

Bitch and *Bastard* alliterate the moments
I'm too pissed from getting licked to pray;

yet sorry is as sorry does. And now the rub:
"Son, have you been impure?"

I conjure words for the occasion of sin:
alley, fire escape, aftermath.

My skin is crawling with it.
"C'mon, boy, commandments ten and eight.

Down there, the spot, the hidden place.
How many times? No *interruptus.*"

Dear God
wants out, out of this house.

The brothers are too far gone to count.
The profile is nodding. The nightshirt laughs.

I can make out the mouth, opening, closing,
teeth, tongue, the nightcap breath.

"How many times, exactly, down below?"
He reads my mind like Tarot.

Communion Partners

(For Philip DeLucia)

These infrequent photographs you send
remind me that twenty years
now separate First Holy Communion partners
and two bearded men on a lakeshore.

You have always taken symbolic photographs:
the sun at our backs in Acadia,
singing about the Quebec women
and throwing our bourbon in the bay—

not the last time we'd squander what we'd paid for;
I, naked in a window seat;
you and Mike Strater loving the G sisters.
Your eye is hard and practiced

these days, and sometimes cunning.
It returns me again to the day we tried,
as boys, to gulp down salvation
which we lived with, like a bad marriage,

until we could no longer.
Who are those boys of beatific face,
steepled hands, festooned with rosaries
and scapulars, dressed like businessmen?

Behind them, the Infant of Prague sits
on His little shelf beneath a white lambrequin;
and little girls, in virginal lace and taffeta,
kneel, full of grace, the Lord with them,

awaiting the advent of archangels.
We believed, yet twenty years later
we are the only witnesses to our martyrdom,
never patient or humble enough to invest

our hard-bought grace. And this last batch—
we stand like statues beneath the sun
on the lake shore, breaking bread, drinking wine—
they've convinced me we're not such fools,

simply older, that success and failure
never mattered from the start.
Benediction was never a question.
Look at your photographs: rife with hosts.

CONFIRMATION

Sister Simon grilled us
for weeks on the questions
the Bishop might ask at random.

I memorized the principle parts of the Mass,
the sacred vessels, Liturgical
colors, commemorations,

the stational churches of Rome.
But the Bishop asked nothing,
gave but a dry slap and palsied stamp of chrism.

I remember only that his name was Thomas,
that his green miter shook
as he asked what name I had chosen.

My Godfather wore a white tie
and clamped my shoulder. Suddenly
a soldier in The Army of Christ,

I couldn't stop thinking of the girls in my class:
their long straight hair and consecrated bodies.
I had taken the name of a man

who became King of France at age fifteen
and led two crusades to the Holy Land.
What did I know

of how men fought and loved?
At the party, I was given money.
Aunts kissed me. Uncles shook my hand

and coaxed me into a shot of whiskey.
All I wanted was to be alone.
In the home movies, I'm a sweet boy

in red blazer, holding a bottle
of Lord Calvert,
everyone about me laughing.

KYRIE

Dumbly I toe my mark,
body possessed of a bad boy's soul,
hoping the strained mercy

of Christ's wife will not crack
like a stick cross my cheek
as I pretend not to know what I know best,

having secretly read my sister's books
and have more words haunting my head
than these experts tattlers

drawing page upon perfect page
of Jesuits at Offertory
in purple vestments.

I've had truck with the devil,
she charges, raven-eyed, gorgeous:
wimple and jackboot oxfords,

black hose, big rosary.
The blackboards circle with my penitent script—
I will not be a vile boy—

chalk dust gagging me,
my fists white.
Her stealth takes my breath,

but truly I cannot check the smile
that steals to my lips on the lane from my soul
as I pray for deliverance, cocking

an ear to the drunks on Flavel Street,
hailing me with empty pints
against the black iron grate.

I Will Mark the Tattler

Paired in gender and drayage,
we come like a twenty mule team,

marching along the black stone wall
that rises against Larimer to bar the convent.

Some hold hands, veiled in the steeple
shadow that stretches the city block.

My cheeks are raw, ill with this season
of beatings and offering-it-up.

There is treachery in the cloak room
and lavatories, in the choir loft

and cracked concrete schoolyard
at recess. I am a horse

they wish to stone, obsessed
by contrition. My nubile soul

is drawn in a pucker, point and drag,
reined in and out by German Sisters

of Divine Providence.
My hate is quicksilver, slew-footed,

a tiny hymn and praise,
a conjecture at the world.

When this line breaks, *hell*
and *damn* are all I'll know.

THE HOLLOW

The old Italian people had a word
for it that sounded like *hollow*,
but with more *hole*, more *woe*
in it—like *holy*:

Bassa La Vallone.
I could not pronounce it,
but it's where I went when I wanted
to be alone despite warnings

of snakes and Spacaluccio,
the monster that lived beneath Meadow Street
Bridge, spanning the Hollow,
and fed on disobedient children.

My woods, a swath of sumac
and crabapples stuck to the shoulder
of Negley Run, was wedged between
cliffs of mixed hungers: black and immigrant.

They fought with rocks and sticks, and screamed
across the abyss at each other, over tops
of trees, under which I huddled, skinning
for a bow and arrows with my first knife

the slender sumac trunk and branches.
In the Hollow the hoods built tree houses
to take their girls—
those black-lashed blondes (*hard,*

my mother called them), Jesus,
that made the green about me flutter:
girls who'd scab with broken bottles
homemade tattoos into their boyfriends' biceps—

a cross with a tongue of flame in each right angle;
then initials, *L.A.*, for Larimer Avenue—
and fry the squirrels they killed with BBs.
What was I doing there—drawn incessantly

deeper into the white gleaming green,
drinking water from a stone,
not getting in from the rain nor making a sound,
eating only the tiny apples

that tasted so much of a foreign tongue?
When I emerged from the thicket,
fathers were just arriving home from work;
traffic was picking up.

Walking along the Run,
I heard car doors slamming
up and down Collins Avenue,
then my name coming at me

from my mother, on the porch
with my father. I hesitated
before allowing myself to be seen.
Things would be changing soon.

I knew. But nothing
had then yet changed,
not at that minute,
that last minute when I didn't know

who I was or what I'd be—
only that there were two worlds:
one of *I*, one of *they*,
and that I was the one.

SISTER

In Mother House dotage
Sister natters at doilies,
knitting one, pearling two.
I learned to count by her lash.
No ether, only Sister
wielding her cat o'nine
with one wedded hand.

When we learned to stuff our pants
with Spellers, she had us strip,
our bird-like privates compelled
against her workbench as she leapt
buttock to buttock—as if playing
a xylophone. The Savior
splayed on his wooden knick-knack
between the Phoenician alphabet
and poster of four food groups.
Some of the boys blubbered.

Home, I practiced my numbers,
sat through dinner on burning loins.
In the convent kitchen, Sister crouched
with the others over boiled meat;
then proceeded in lockstep to her cell,
a thousand rosary beads clattering
to the cold as the nuns disrobed.

Sister scraped clean her skin
with razors, swabbed with Witch
Hazel and Iodine, blacked
boots and laid out her pitch linen.
Hair cropped, naked, white,
she looked like pictures of Vichy girls,
hitched to ox-carts, heads shaved
for taking Nazi lovers.

ALL HALLOW'S EVE

Dressed as our patron saints,
we entered the convent through its scullery:
stainless steel, white vaults, vessels
dangling from black hooks.

Then into the marble corridor,
off which the sick chamber bore,
where we cowed, attendant to the next
click of Sister Daria's fingers.

The walls respirated with vespers.
Camphor escaped the jamb beyond
which Sister Clement was dying.
Her room was overheated,

the curtain thrown back
to let through the soaped window
the end of the day's gray light.
At the headboard

stood an orange air cylinder.
Wearing a blue robe, hands braided
with a tiny-beaded pink rosary,
its Christ silver on a pink cross,

the ancient nun angled into a mound
of bedclothes. No wimple, but a thin
veil pinned to her head, faded gray
hair misted at her temples.

Prodded by Daria, as we paraded
around the bed, we one at a time
approached Sister Clement:
Stephen, Joan, Brdigette, Paul,

on and on, an entire roll of martyrs,
tortured, dead in droves, without complaint.
At each proclamation, she smiled
and nudged sweets across the spread.

When I stepped up and whispered,
Joseph, she dug her hand in mine
and sighed until she moaned.
I had disguised myself as a just man.

Had we been alone, I might have asked
to touch her hair, confessed
I'd been thinking only of the shoplifted
Tareytons I'd smoke that night vampiring

through the streets. I might have cried.
Instead, with the lump of chocolate
she'd stuck in my fist, I spun,
suddenly nauseated at the room's red heat

and my horsehair beard. Thrashing
with my staff through my fellow saints,
I rushed into the convent garden.
In the house across the avenue,

the whores were just waking,
goblins already on their porch,
trick or treating.
Chocolate dripped from my hand.

FORBES FIELD

We sit in right—
the seats are blue—over which

Ruth's last home run still rockets ...
Vendors wander cold night empty rows.

In the bullpen, relievers huddle in a murder,
like crows, black-jacketed, blowing

into their fists, no one throwing.
Ronnie Kline and Al McBean pass a cigarette.

My father and a buddy from the mill
talk about 1960: Terry's pitch

Mazeroski launched over the scoreboard.
I sip my dad's coffee and hope

the game will never end.
Clemente's on-deck.

I lean dangerously out over the warning
track—*Arriba*,

Roberto—praying
for the two-out-lightning

that will bring him to the plate.
The smell of coal lifts off the river.

Wind stiffens the flag above the ivy
in left, night beyond the wall parched

by stack-fire and a thousand boom crane spindles.
In Hazelwood, the deadman's shift listens

to the game on the radio and makes steel
for the new ball park. Billy

Virdon broken-bats an inside curve to short.
The Pirates disappear from the dugout.

THE WITCH

She stood for what we did
on broken glass in her soot yard

on Shakespeare Street—
ours to stone on the way to break

windows in vacant foundries,
the pall of sweets from National Biscuit

glazing each pile of bricks and twisted metal.
Our favorite games were killing.

Our favorite books were death.
It had been beaten into us:

God is Love.
Not the parched face and gnarled

capes, jittering in the nude
sky, we could not see trying

to touch us for the blood in our eyes.
Nor could we hear the monody

from the impoverished lips of madness
eloped with before our births—

only her toothless incantations
of *stop* and *please*, muted

by the buckeyes rifling
off her one-room haunted house.

THE DEATH OF EAST LIBERTY

The Catholic had been assassinated,
his Frontier swept away

by glass and brick dust.
The wrecking ball emptied the sky like an atom bomb.

Half the voters could not speak English
to save their homes. They spit

on the sidewalk and cursed the tinhorn
politicos they'd stood at the polls for

to keep their kids working.
Women lit candles and went to pieces

with their hands. The men sat in rubble
and wept with the jackhammers.

Trees were plucked and houses
bowled over like fleeced drunks.

In the end they moved, took the five grand
their lives had been bountied for

and a made a face of beginning.
But demolition had crept into the bloodline,

a reliance on silence and breaking to chastise love.
Memory became the abstraction of vendetta.

Italians went to their graves without speaking,
wholly terrified of America.

THE STRIKE BABY

(For my Mother & Father & Marie)

Eleven dollars a week
unemployment

and I wasn't getting pregnant.
When I did

your father went on strike.
We were renting from

Nick and Ida Santilli.
They said forget about the rent

until the baby comes.
You were due.

Your father was on strike.
Then winter came;

and, my God, the snow.
The 1950 snow:

everybody called it
the big snow.

I baked bread.
We bought produce from the huckster.

Daddy painted Abe
and Lena Vento's house.

They bought us a crib,
so we asked them

to be Godparents.
The days Daddy got paid,

he brought home
a twenty cent pie.

It cost a hundred and ten
dollars to have a baby:

nine months care
and delivery,

calcium and vitamin pills.
Two days after

you were born,
the strike ended.

THE BRIDGE TO NOWHERE

What I imagined of my sister's dates
were scrubbed young men shooting
to their feet, holding doors,
long dark movie aisles,
then a coke or something.

Boyfriends seemed exacted from her life
of books. But not just any liar
gets a good girl to mount the Bridge
to Nowhere, a span simply aborted
mid-construction three hundred feet
in midair above the Monongahela.

I never pictured Marie without her glasses,
begging of risk revelation,
standing on the half-bridge
with a thin-lipped Irish boy who fed her
beer and cigarettes. All she knew
of him were his Princeton and penny loafers.
He knew patently nothing of her,
least of all what it meant to be
a good girl on the brink
who has heard the voice of rapture
whispering: *This is how to fall*—
into the river of little fire
like fallen stars dissolving
in the industrial murk.

When she crept back into the house
no one knew her long hair and naked face—
the life, still cradled in her hands,
she'd all night lived above the river.

DARIA

It was always from the same daydream
of the schoolhouse falling
from the weight of flame that I was yanked
to my feet by a sideburn

by a one-armed nun who had
where there should have been a shoulder
a black shelf to which was pinned the gold
band wedding her to the Son of Man.

If I caught her eye, she'd bat me over,
then any boy who laughed,
boxing our ears with stump and fist,
pinning a whole choir against the board,

croaking out *The Sanctus*
as she finished us with sucker punches.
The girls she simply mortified.
She claimed she knew what we were thinking.

It was then with ardor we thought of flesh,
the pictures ripped from the barber's washroom.
Even the half-robed and pilloried martyrs
occasioned our pent blood to rise—

the ubiquitous plush of the virgin's shoulder
going down in the snarl of wild dogs.
But there was little heart to our lust,
only the confusion of not knowing

how long we'd have in our bodies.
The year she taught us the nouns, *semen*
and *ovum*, I fought an older boy
in a foundry lot who accused my parents

of using their bodies to have me—
the first time I'd ever used my fist on a face.
Sister Daria picked slag chips from my hands
with tweezers and let me cuss as she rubbed them

with alcohol. "This is nothing,"
she hissed, then emptied the entire bottle.
When the school burnt—perhaps
because of that one unsnuffed butt

in the condemned lyceum—
we realized Purgatory had all along
resided where we'd been sitting
in fear of immolation.

Throwing third graders to firemen below,
Sister Daria died in a window.
The day of her Requiem,
in cassock and surplice, I swept

wedding rice from the church steps.
Even then I thought of things forbidden:
the bride and groom,
the bedroom door closing.

A Player Without a Game

Dropping out of the clouds
into the silver above my hometown,
my eye from the airplane
has somehow trained itself
to light upon Southside Stadium,

a caved-in cinder surrounded
by a cadre of mills and slag heaps
where, on Saturday nights,
hunkered into my shoulder pads at halftime,
I sat beneath its rickety stands

and studied my coach
for the slightest sign of disbelief.
Above us we could hear the people
banging up and down the planks
and the band playing the fight song

over and over as we formed
a great circle around our coach,
each of us straining to touch him
as we prayed to Our Lady of Victory.
That I would someday see this man

drunk and silly on a corner
close to the stadium and he would speak
as if we'd been boys together
never occurred to me. But then
my life had the perfect lines

and identical faces of a cut diamond.
When we lost a game, we mourned,
never really apprehended by our sorrow,
but merely players suddenly without a game.
We'd bribe a wino outside the Anchor Tavern

to buy us a gallon of cheap wine,
drink it crouched with the bums in the dank freeze
of the train tunnel next to the gym;
then barge into the dance, hair still wet
from the showers, frozen

on our necks and foreheads.
There I'd watch the others fall
in love under the hoops and make out
in the bleachers, listen to the sad velvet
music, then rush to slow-drag

any girl who would lift her face to mine
across the saw-dusted boards
to *High on a Hill* and *Harlem Nocturne*.
Smelling her hair and sweater,
feeling her thin fingers across my shoulders,

I'd close my eyes and sing in her ear.
Now, as my life flies through the air
with me inside it, I am given
a tiny window to scrutinize the world
that extorted my boyhood. Typically,

my double-crossing eye unhinges itself
and hurries to places that no longer exist.
And I feel alone like the boy in his first suit—
after the game, after the dance, drunk
from warm sweet blood-red wine.

LET THE BOY TRY

Sitting in Dickie's T-bird
with his dazzling redhead wife,

I'm wondering what it's like
to drive a car and have a woman.

Behind us, a boy is loaded
into a wagon that will climb Mount Carmel

where we'll leave him. I don't remember
what I was wearing, but I got the news

at Mellon Park, drinking Iron City quarts
with Gazalian and Park Joe who got mad

trying to teach me pinochle.
Clyde Wible, wrecked on a ping-pong table,

slurred over and over, "Let the Boy Try."
I started home, feeling oddly sorry

for myself—a spike hole in my hand,
football practice at dawn the next morning,

then the wake—whistling
the score to *A Band of Angels*.

OCTOBER

Waiting for the 7:10 Bronx Express,
a man finds a '41 baseball card
of Joe DiMaggio in his topcoat lining

causing him to weep all day at his desk.
His wife wakes alone. Watching *Niagara*
on The Million Dollar Movie

she undresses and hugs herself
between freezing sheets, remembering
tiny mouths of blue milk that blessed

and emptied the last summer before the war.
The man drags home, spurred
like the quiet Clipper, after fighting

a World Series crowd and finds his wife
painting her nails in the bay window,
hair still blonde as boned ash.

He knows the grace it takes to hit in 56
straight, to be more than a ballplayer.
"I wanted it to go on forever,"

DiMag once said wistfully of the streak,
as though he'd not gone far enough
in jolting epiphany.

Seeing her husband's silver hair
and Sicilian jaw, the woman too
knows they are commemorative

of doomed love whispering beneath
the onslaught of autumn brilliance:
Nothing is ever lost or forgotten.

COURTING THE CHATHAM GIRLS

As we stripped in the hedge-rowed commons,
the tree-topped moon dispatched us

like thieves among statues and crypts
of old Fellows on which we'd draped our clothes.

We'd lie naked on the lawn, smoking,
watching the chandeliers wink

from the faculty mansions;
listen to the restive setters, and a capella

auguring Sabbath from the hill-stoned chapel.
Then we slipped like knives into Chatham

fountain, sunk to its marble floor, swimming
silently stealing nothing until surfacing

when the girls, humming with Vespers, pleated
skirts and blazers brushing the boxwood

that concealed us, promenaded toward gleaming
quarters to bathe, slip into summer gowns

and brush their long hair with measured strokes.
That we lingered too long imagining them

was our only indiscretion. For the blue light
wailed and we were scraping up a slate wall

roped with honeysuckle, racing
down Fifth Avenue, naked outlaws,

faster than the cops the rich had hired to keep us
from their girls and out of their water.

DON JUAN

I was then 16 in love.
About me was a loosing of instinct.

Out of coffee houses wafted reefer
and sandalwood. On Walnut Street,

Flower Children flashed the police peace signs.
I loafed with hoods who beat up hippies.

We drank Don Juan a *runner*, paid
with the first unending chug, grubbed

for us out of the State Store.
I gagged it down, hating its gut-rusting

luke-warmth, its irrevocability.
Girls nailed shut their sashes at my passing.

Fathers trained steak knives on me.
I was really a nice boy, but couldn't stop

bashing windshields. By that time
I had been cut or worse, lying

on the cobbles crying because I had forgotten
the way home. "You son-of-a-bitches,"

I raved at the streetlights,
as I'd secretly read true rebels grieved,

knowing the girl I was choking for
would never be mine, the girl I fell for

because she was wrong for me.
There were songs about it: *Baby,*

I ain't your kind, and the like—
far tenderer. But, with a mouthful of blood

and wine, I knew nothing
about having a *Baby.*

Those freaks—they'd sashay by me,
hung up on the Walnut sign-pole.

Their hair and clothes—
they were so beautiful.

"Man," they'd say, smiling,
forking up those Vs, "peace."

I'd whisper, "peace,"
lift two fingers, "love."

Wrestling Practice: Sunday Morning, 1969

Embarking from the city bus
back seat, stenched
with last night's love,
I cross frozen Fifth Avenue,
cut through the courtyard
of the Christian Brothers' House,
with its fabled stores of black beer
and celibacy. In the quadrangle,
like a missile poises a statue of wizened
Jesus. I take my place in the cold
effluvia of the locker room, strip
and slip into the rubber body bag.
1969: I have the hunger
of citrus-fed wrestlers who bread crave
and the surcease of laxatives, spitting,
nocturnal purge and sleepwalk to the scales,
praying to make weight come the match.

* * *

The blue and gold mats are stiff
when we hit the cellar room for warm-up,
the boiler's heat high-turned to smelt us.
Brother Coach, three hundred pounds
of concupiscence clubbed
into a black mat-length habit,
has been to Mass already,
his breakfast of Eucharist.
For the hell of it, he pummels the walls
with his massive forearms, and sings
Ave Maria until the icons jitter.

* * *

The room begins to stink:
fifty Catholic bodies at war.
BTUs rise off my opponent as I ride him,
his sweat running down my arms,
in my face and mouth; his lousy aroma,
cauliflower ears, scabbed sideburns,
feline tongue. I move among
the stations of the *Cross-face, Guillotine,*
Double-heel, Sit-out, Whizzer , Switch,
Half-nelson, Syracuse, Crucifix.

* * *

In my throat I taste the bloody
icicles of reproach, trip with the rest
dripping, blind upstairs to the empty school
for laps and cals, time for one precious
half-second to duck into the head,
kneel at the piss trough,
cough up the quid of loss.
Water we may not swallow.

* * *

The chill marble yields not to our hands,
feet, faces as we contort against it—
burnished in the ken of its half-century
of secret boys marching hallward
into what they believe is the future.
Brother goosesteps among us, uttering
in Latin commands that send us lurching
to the next set, chanting like monks
the count; then into neck bridges, bowed
crotch up (altars) teetering
on toe-tips and crown. Sweat
inscribes the floor. Brother barks:

"Two more minutes." Then: "Two more
minutes," after that. On throughout
*The Litany of the Most Precious Blood
of Jesus,* followed by *Psalm 69—*
Deign, O God, to rescue me;
O Lord, make haste to help me—
our skulls splitting with upside-down
invocation, spilling all desire—we bleat
in pain—save to be up and, at command,
running .....

* * *

Brother routes us along the first floor,
then four flights up to the fourth. Down
again, up again—indefinitely, past
portraits of our famous grads:
All-Americans, physicians,
poets, politicians.
With glassed airs of achievement,
they look down upon on our shambling
The heavyweights puke in the stairwells.

* * *

The clock sweats out each minute.
As we run by Brother he shouts, in turn,
Dago, Snowflake, Hunky, Kraut—
his way of exacting virtue of ancestry.
I run in dread fog, the counters of my psyche
registering a semblance of hour and date,
my narrative of effacement:
Make weight, make weight...

* * *

72

In the trophy case, agleam
like the lights of prom cars,
the cruciform empty jersey
of our martyr dreams.
Danny Rafalko, number 63, baby-
faced, cock-strong from Lawrenceville—
sweetest kid ever to wear the colors.
Wrestling 165, he got thrown in
with the real animals—who lived for it:
scarred, shaved heads to butt with,
huge veiny arms; out-there
killers who signed up for Special
Forces and came home crazy.
Rafalko would end up street-fighting—
he only wrestled to keep in shape
for football—couldn't keep himself
from punching after he was pinned.
It took Brother, the Ref, and two seniors
to haul him back to the bench.
A year after he graduated,
you could check him out any night
on Butler Street, along the river—
he had grown long his hair, a goatee—
unemployed, bum SATs, bombed
on malt liquor and a couple numbers,
waiting on the draft board.
I'd honk on the way home from practice.
He'd amble to the car, and knuckle
me through the open window,
smile: "Fuck deferment."

* * *

Who knew what was coming?
TET? Hue? Who knew?
Brother. He'd say it:

Gooks. Zipperheads.
He had rooted *Japs* out of tunnels in Saipan
and still kept his hair in a Parris Island.
It was guts Brother loved. No matter
how rough he was, you still wanted him
to love you. I'd witnessed him muttering
in front of Rafalko's jersey. Because
I'd spied him, he slapped me in the face—
not hard, but the kind of Confirmation
whack you take from the Bishop.
He uttered my name—
tacked a *Y* on the end of it.

* * *

We end the workout with wind sprints.
"Twenty, well to well," Brother yells.
"Then take it in. One dogger
and you do it all over again."
He claps and a pair of us slaps
the marble; then another
and another until the hall echoes
with flap and heaving. Like starvelings
glowering over the last haunch, we eye
one another as though among us
is a Judas, a breaker, without the will for it.
All we have is the illusion of our bodies,
Brother insisting there's something extra
pounding in us we've yet to discover,
something he can extort with a look and shiver.
And when we have run our twenty,
we are made to run twenty more.

* * *

74

We quail before the last labor:
heaving the mat through the winter
storm to the gym for next day's match
with The School for the Deaf.
It takes the entire team to heft,
rolled like three tree trunks in cylinders,
reeking like an abattoir,
the accretion of all manner of boys
yeared into it. Wind-shorn
sleet flaks us, icing into spikes
our boiling sweat. If one falls,
we're all done for, so there's no quitting.
God, we're not even up to prayer.
Brother's left us crossed with this.
He's in the Brother House, drinking beer.

* * *

The locker room, a shipwreck, smells
of turned earth. Cramped. Bodies
jostling to strip. Water streams
out beneath the rubber sweats—
I think of *Catch 22*, Snowden's guts
spilling out of his flak jacket—
puddling the chipped tiles.
Lock chains rattle. Doors blow open.
Brother, leading the wind, reappears.
He proclaims: "Despair,
because of heat or cold or hunger,
is unbecoming," that "with a double-
hernia and nothing for a jock but a peanut
shell and rubber band," he went both ways
for a season in Canada.

He takes out his teeth, kicks over
the trash can, jacks up against a locker
the biggest boy he can lay hands to.
No one speaks. Some drop
naked to the floor for pushups.
Our anorexic 88 takes to the whirlpool
to boil away a pound or two.
When Brother departs, a centerfold
makes its way around the room.
She seems a dear chaste angel.
I feel nothing for her,
but veneration.
Upperclassmen seize the best showers.
Four years as hunger artists
have stretched them into haters.
No room in them for anything,
but what's left to them of their bodies—no soul
for music, not even for a girl's love.
I slump in a metal chair beneath a fizzing
shower, unconsciously soaping, until
the hot water runs cold.
The scale squeals as boy after boy, dragging
across the metal integers the heavy
stylus, climbs on and off.
I'd rather weigh in private
the sacred occasion of what I am
at heart, stripped of every pretense,
but survival. I mount it like I might kiss
a girl: breath held high, arms
crooked at the elbows, palms down
ahead of me like a sacristan awaiting
his confessor's stole and whisper.
The locker room's lone toilet
never stops running.

* * *

Sleet has way given to snow and thunder,
the High Mass bells of Saint Paul's.
I am four pounds under
and this, along with the snow,
amounts to happiness.
I walk into Cathedral Pharmacy,
sit at the counter and order toast
from a girl wearing a blue hair band
in her long yellow hair.
Her voice is my hunger.
As she butters the toast,
she glances dreamily at the snow curtaining
the plate glass windows fronting Fifth.
No one else is in here.
They're all in church listening
to the Bishop serenade Jesus.
Slowly, I eat the toast, unspeakably
delicious, gazing at the girl
as she studies the snow.
It's alright, this one time,
if I have more—this pittance.
I'll go home and spit it off.

Three Rivers

(For David and Philip)

From where the incline perched us
above the congress of rivers,
the sheer immensity of the city

made us laugh. We imagined
that between the two worlds
we were suspended was a safe place

to calibrate how far we'd come,
how far there was to go.
Below: the cracked, rude aggregate

of the Southside where miles of mills
walled rivers from streets
with devout engines of steel.

Old mill-hands lined the wharf nightly,
nimbused by the glow of each ladled heat,
fishing for the sinister Steeltown carp,

watching shifts stack into lifetimes.
Dangling in mid-air, toasting
one another with rotgut bourbon,

we were hoodwinked by our world,
eyes on the rivers commingling
at the famous Point. For each of us,

we dreamed, was a river—
Allegheny, Monongahela,
Ohio—and, like those rivers,

there was the illusion of triune destiny,
water enough to buoy three lifetimes.
We would never part.

Their fathoms willed us to aim at fire,
thread ourselves into a birthright ringed
with steel and lonely men fishing.

The future would sturdy us by risk
and measurement: a length of cable,
narrow rails, a row of lights, an incline.

This would always be our town.
We would build houses on industrial cliffs
above the Point, and enter them

through the guts of the mountain,
testifying to the way
three rivers come together.

THE DAY I WAS BORN: THE 1972 DRAFT LOTTERY

I cower in the snow storm: destiny—
what my dad means when he says,
"When's your number's up, it's up."
"Thirty-three," I whisper aloud,

let my tongue take in a wafer of snow.
Waiting for my girl in front of Sacred Heart,
I smoke Newports, occasionally clubbing
the dash to keep the radio playing

Instant Karma. In the church
the faithful consecrate to Jesus
in the spirit of reparation
First Friday devotions.

She's been crying.
When she slides into the car,
she throws her arms around me:
"We'll go to Canada."

Though that's not what I'm thinking,
I say, "Okay," and like children
with a simple plan, we're relieved.
Everything will be alright;

we can still get married.
In uniform blazer and plaid jumper,
pitifully thin like pictures of Biafrans,
beautiful in a terrible way, she huddles

against me, threading my arm
with fraught nail-bitten fingers.
On the backs of her hands are black
magic-markered peace signs, faded

from the nuns' forced scrubbing, but still indelible.
The streetlights come on early.
Squirrel Hill, in the snowy smoked light,
blurs on this Jewish Sabbath-eve.

Black-robed rabbis, long square beards
tattering white, rock on bus islands.
Flapping with books, yarmulkeed students
run for the bus. Shop-owners

pull their shades. An invisible sun
skids off Murray Avenue.
In Weinstein's we order motzah ball soup,
hot tea, share a blintz—all the money

we have; then stroll through the Head Shop's
black-lit world of other: pipes,
clips, skins, beads, iron-ons,
the kaleidoscopic raiment of Aquarius.

Hippies in wire-rims and Captain America
shirts skate along, unconsumed
by what consumes me—a simple number: 33.
I realize I have no ideology.

I think of my family—
how we'll not talk. All my life,
it seems, the war has been there, spying
on me from the eye of our Zenith.

It never looked like the movies:
less method, no plot, simply filmic
vignettes of helmetless corpsmen
with Red Cross arm bands, hovering

with morphine and plasma over
the booby-trapped, holding a cigarette
to the face of the immemorable,
yet familiar, dragging on it too—

somewhere obviously a camera
making it all seem …
the way it must be thousands of miles away,
waiting to return to what never existed.

The car is cauled in snow. Inside
we abandon ourselves like real lovers
to clutch and promise, pressing our teeth
together. In this opaque, everything stills.

Bus brakes exhale. Salt trucks strafe.
Streetlights trace star-scapes on the windshield.
I place about her bare shoulders my army jacket.
She weeps and asks me what I'm thinking.

"About you," I whisper, but this isn't true.
I'd been pondering what might protect me,
and in my ignorance conjured a gun
to fill the space between me and what awaited

with enough fire to put the future in its grave.
"About you," I repeat, twist the key,
try the wipers. It's late.
We're both in trouble.

MENDICANT ON A BRIDGE

From desperate reaches above the Atlantic,
I send my mother letters detailing
the etymology of barnacle and sea cucumber,
subtle notes of piers and bridges.

She reads these at kitchen table,
in house coat and slippers,
drinking tea like a vexed Chinawoman
attempting to pinpoint the digressions

of my cursive hand. She wonders why
I cannot walk a straight line.
I describe unfamiliar terrain.
She twirls the globe to find me—

never there. The world turns me
sadly over like a boy on a spit.
At day's end she's tired and elusive.
Care has worn her like an old coat.

On a whim she drops to hands and knees,
drags a rag skeptically across the tile floor.
Have I punished her too long
with my ceaseless hunger, ignoring

this kitchen demon for a phantom woman?
My letters are elegies to a girl
leaning cockily on the fender
of a two-toned roadster, with a rumble seat,

parked on the Hoeveler Street Bridge—1937.
She wears a look I suspect I've seen,
but never recognized.
I alone possess this portrait

of her secret girlhood. My secret
mother, long-haired, lovely,
not so practical; and, as I am
now, mendicant on a bridge.

Here there is a breaking of destiny.
We travel together in these letters:
to the Pacific, the Aegean;
any sea; a new conception,

a more harrowing gestation.
Tell them not to search
the land for me, Mother.
I am gone

to long-haired girls of 1937,
a bridge still standing
uncrashed into the Hollow.
I'll bleed the stone womb for water.

Epistle to Sal

Sal:

Courage is sometimes a mirage—not a quality of the hero, but an aberration. Children are taught early to break hearts with bravery, and later how to kill and die because of it. I've been reading *johnny got his gun*, something I've put off for years and, now reading it, it's no wonder; Emerson, too, for the first time in my nearly thirty years. Prior to two weeks ago, I'd assiduously avoided him. There'd be no transcending for me. See how I sidestep difficult writers (Lack of courage?)? Emerson says "self-trust is the essence of heroism," then goes on to say there's nothing logical about it, but who doesn't admire a hero when one crops up? But you and I have 142 years more in the way of perspective than Ralph—and Vietnam to boot. We're not heroes. We've escaped the wars. The man you saw immolated in the car crash— let's pray for him, but in this case, what's the point of mourning? The key phrase in your letter is: "I knew I couldn't do a thing." Your breast-beating in front of the crucifix was appropriate. We Catholics are urged to seek absolution for every plague ever conjured in the universe. After all, we anoint our babies lightning-fast so they won't be tortured for a trespass which occurred millennia ago, if at all. Jesus was a realist. He wasn't just running a scam. If He really was God, He proved it—at least according to what records we've retained. I realize this is digressive, but we've talked about all this before, even studied it together. But when have you ever heard Jesus referred to as a hero? Timing is everything. If He were around today, He'd probably be a millionaire and wouldn't have to be crucified. Or He'd sell his story to the networks and endear Himself to the masses in fourteen prime-time installments. Okay. Back to Emerson: "Greatness once and forever has done with opinion." Feel snug in this. You're no coward. I've got one beer and I'm not going to drink it till five. This is the kind of solemn promise I make myself when I'm alone, trying to work.

The Fire on Callowhill

Dreaming in my old bed:
broken glass, conspiring hush,
snarled whisper; cadged butt,
an arsonist's pitch-soaked rag;

the private cognition of flame
imagining my face in the cradle.
This, the night of my birth, thirty
times itself contiguous, three

decades since this house celebrated me.
My mother has told me how I hurried
from the womb, since wished
a continuum of birth nights

where sleep curls my tongue round natal
vowels and hot nights light me like candles—
more fire than I have breath for,
a cake big as Purgatory.

My own legs must run me from this red-
frosted nightmare of engines and sirens
wailing. I rouse my wife,
navigate the tricky hall by rote

to my parents' empty glowing bed.
It's the five-story walk-up, condemned,
built with WPA money; a marvel
of brick and masonry—1936

chiseled into the southwest granite soldier
juncturing Callowhill and Mellon.
Smoke glooms. Flame shades
the sills like laughing ghosts.

Piked and battle-axed firemen dance
in and out like carpenter ants, rappelling
the walls, spinning ladders to the eaves,
scaling the pyric eye which hides itself

till the last, then springs—orange
gash—crowning the rat-trap.
The entire neighborhood—Black,
Latin, Jew—throngs the street,

snaked with hoses and life-lines,
under a sky colored wolf, gasping
like a circus crowd. Transfigured,
aged, integrated around the occasion

of fire, they will fight to the last—
with garden hoses, if need be.
But who will tell them they've been good
at living, at outlasting

what my generation calls Karma?
The moon preens, nearly full,
minutely shaded by a black sliver
of firmament. Mercury

in retrograde confounds reason.
The ravaged brick husk fizzes
and throws occasional sparks
into the street where firemen lie,

swallowing Red Cross coffee
and doughnuts—their job finished,
my wish made. Tomorrow
this occurrence, already dovetailing

into past, will return to dream,
metamorphosed by the tales
of what turned us out of sleep
one blazing night in July.

Some day, in our ancient bed,
Joan and I will recall the night. "Remember
the fire of your thirtieth birthday?"
she'll ask for no reason.

And I'll be left scratching
my gray beard, trying like dream
to recollect fire in the basement
of my memory.

SOFTBALL

Boxed by a cyclone fence,
the field perches on a milltown bluff.
In left are apartments, blackened
from eighty years of ore dust.
A man on the third floor,
drinking a can of Iron,
looks out over the rusty backstop.
He never misses an inning.
The whole neighborhood is laid off,
taking it on by getting old.

The game starts with both teams,
shoulder to shoulder, walking the field
for rocks and glass. No grass
to keep down the dust, the city
rolls it with oil that wells up
around the plate on a hot day.

We play once real athletes
who let go their bodies for love
and doubling out on the Open Hearth.
Now they're broke, can't run,
but still have good eyes
and can kill the ball.

We end up losing
because we're small and out of town.
Our pluck is outdated,
uniforms too nice. After nine
we know a lot about them.
A loss would make them mean.
The know the mills will never start up again.
In a fight we'd be pushovers.

This is nothing like hardball
where the mound is further
from home, the bases longer.
The ball is big and friendly.
No one strikes out.
The only distant thing is the past.

The Toy Warehouse

(For David Friday)

The morning sun in our faces,
David and I drive to work
along Allegheny River Boulevard.
Once into what city calls country,

the black sunken mills give way
to marinas strung with pleasure boats.
We have time for two or three cigarettes,
coffee, catch some scores,

a little music on the radio.
Through the windshield,
it's all out there, green, glistening,
and there are things we think we know—

a way through all the bullshit.
The warehouse clock thuds me in for the day.
I buy a box of Junior Mints
and begin scavenging sets

out of fragmented pieces: disembodied
heads, decapitated bodies,
thousands of wheels, blocks, cogs
and spindles that fit nothing—

the refuse of a broken little world
I must all day make matter.
The grey metal racks of inventory
stretch row after row, a hundred

yards long, fifty feet to the silver
insulation packed between girders,
where in a hideout of boxes
filled with dolls that talk and wet themselves

I smoke and read *The Idiot*.
Myshkin, I muse, *for Christ's sake,*
break a few jaws,
take no more shit, kiss her.

The hard-hatted pickers, filling
orders, glide in hydraulic forklifts,
up and down about me, squirting
one another with water pistols.

Each has a favorite toy; theft is popular.
They keep their headgear on during lunch
in the fly-filled break-room, drink
coffee from smoking thermoses.

David wanders down from his station
in hobbies. Sitting on a bay
opened for a semi dispatching GI Joe's,
we smoke a roach, buy devilled

crab from Munch's Lunchtruck, kill
the last few minutes before the horn
with cigarettes. I sift through
tiny orphans, educational toys

with Myshkin smiles: the fireman
in search of fire, the mustachioed
police chief locked from his jail,
the spinstered school-marm.

Their enameled fortitude mocks me.
I ransack piles of renegade effects,
trying to reconnect their lives.
How in such carefully packaged

products does separation occur?
Returning to my Pocket Penguin
I await what my Dostoevsky Seminar calls
that *explosive, typically Russian scene*

that will lift Myshkin from his existential mire.
But he continues to stick it out, smiling,
turning the other cheek again
and again. He's a prince.

Quitting time jars me awake, my finger
still sliced in the page that sedated me.
David's finishing up a game of Chess
with Sneak, a guy our age

with a family, who makes extra bread
fencing kiddie pools and Lionel trains.
We keep watch while he smuggles
a load through a back entrance to his car,

then punch out and head for the bar.
Sam and Ann's beer is stunning,
the only benefit so far of being 21.
The guys refer to their wives

as *the Mrs., the little lady,*
the old lady, ball and chain, the boss.
I sort of love these weirdoes,
stealing time from their lives to bitch

it out with the toys at the warehouse.
The jukebox describes: *a man*
with a Union gig,
smashed-up heart,

face like a pig.
The bar is on the river,
hot, summer, still, unnaturally
green and solid. Good and drunk

we goad one another into jumping in.
The sun is behind us. When we walk
onto the dock, we see before going under
carp feeding on our naked shadows.

Beneath there's a clockless kingdom,
a reach of merman hungering
in the river of toy souls.
They have beat it here before us.

When I open my eyes,
we're not all there, just shirts,
names stitched across breast pockets,
twisted in the dock pilings.

III. This Metal

MY FATHER RISING

In Doric beach chair my father reposes,
chiseled against a black vaulted sky.

Today he's reached earth's apogee.
His generation convenes on water—

no matter for architecture.
At his feet, DJ and Katy widen

their flanks like little generals, deploy
barricades north and south, sure

the tide-most sea wall. The storm
bulls in at twenty knots, torching

firmament as far as Loveladies.
Families struggle inland, whole

encampments abandoned, leaving
what can't be carried. The sea banks

through outcropping hills, flooding roads,
swamping dooryards. Sand spins

like sugar. Ghost crabs march
across the dead. The kids bucket

and shovel madly until snatched by their mother,
my sister, from the ramparts.

My father rises, pork-pied, water-crazed,
inscrutable as the prelapsarian

God—the city he underpinned
swallowed—and welcomes

the ocean that's tracked him
across the Atlantic.

UNCLES

I.

My uncles left permanently
for the townships the row-house
on Omega Street where they'd grown up.
With their own hands, they built one-storey
ranches: Formica booths spliced
into breakfast nooks, Madonnas
hutched in masonry grottoes, brick
barbeques. Lazy Susans, intercoms,
Croquet. Trick dogs. Their wives
wore pedal-pushers, and coddled
their cigarettes in leather pouches
with compartments for matches and nail-files.

Sunday, after High Mass and brunch
with the Holy Name Society,
my uncles visited their mother.
They dressed alike, held in their laps
brown pony bottles; and, not saying
a word, sat staring in the sepia
flicker of the gothic Magnavox
until *The Twentieth Century* came on
and Walter Cronkite's Jehovah-like voice
urged them out the door. I crept around
and drank the beer dregged in their bottles.

My father, a millwright on the Open
Hearth, had married one of their sisters.
At family picnics at North Park,
when he was working seven day swing shifts,
my uncles would ring me in the pool,
and hurl me head-first into the deep.
I knew it was something I was supposed
to be able to take. I knew this
from the way they laughed each time
I surfaced, screaming, trying
to get my breath before they were on me again,
their hands like pliers, shaking me
above the water. Trapped
beneath it, waiting to rise again to air—
the water shot through with veins
of light and amniotic pockets
of astral faces—I realized,
even though they loved me,
they would kill me. Only when my mother
lost her temper and jumped in the pool
in her dress, they relented, standing
to their waists—leering Atlases—watching
her carry me, crying, to the blanket.

II.

The curbs outside DeRosa's are lined
with my uncles' late model cars.
Purple flags hang from aerials.
Packed into suits, faces nicked from mid-week
shaves, they stand on the mortuary porch.
Inside a rosary is being said. Across
the street, a man beats a big brown dog.
He shouts at it and punches it in the face.
The dog from its haunches takes it,
never moves except to sidle
when its master starts kicking.
At each strike and whimper, pain
gathers in my uncles' tear-stained faces.
The man lifts the dog by its choke-chain,
twists it tighter and tighter, yanking
the strangling dog to the tips of its back paws
until they are face to face.
Then he breaks
into a laugh
and kisses it.

THIS METAL

Out of this furnace, this metal.
— Thomas Bell, *Out of This Furnace*

Along the rivers' dark green shoulders
stretch miles of empty parking lots
and broken windows.

This is my father's country.
High above Andrew Carnegie's first blast
furnaces, he swung on boom

cranes for forty years with thirty
pounds of steel on his hips.
He saw men die on the open hearth.

A Union man, he was untouchable.
The Slavs couldn't say his name—
called him *Joe Bananas*.

In his retirement, he gardens and cooks
and goes to their funerals.
He has held on all his life,

not talking. When the mill struck
I stole time at his bedside.
I had never seen him sleep.

His repose frightened me: disheveled
hair and empty hands, opened
mouth under which widened a circle

of saliva, his watch and cigarettes
on the nightstand. I contrived noises
to wake him while on the floor below

my mother and sister padded ghost-like.
When he opened his eyes he described
the uncertainty of setting foot in thin air:

"It's not the fall, son, but the sudden stop."
Yesterday he saw a man jump
into the Allegheny. *An old man,*

as described by my seventy year old
father. I imagine him watching
from the rail, shaking his head, muttering

somethin' as the man, who'd beaten him
to the brink, bobbed toward his destination—
a place my father glimpsed often

in his solitary climbs above the now
vanished fire. When we were kids,
he had two suits. Today is a work day.

He is wearing one of them to the funeral.
"How's he taking it?" I ask my mother.
"You know him," she says,

then starts to cry.
He understands. But no one
can get him to talk.

TURNS

Twenty years ago, I raced the curfew
siren home to find a borrowed pistol

in a drawer next to my father's head.
The city on fire, King was dead.

Surrounded by what had been built by slave labor,
we smelled smoke across the river.

The blacks who walked here were daygirls and yardmen
who never lifted their eyes from the street;

and garbage men who crept in and left
slung with our dirt before light singing

hymns my father knew from his pick and shovel days,
humping swing shifts on the Open Hearth,

and moonlighting as a cook at the Kennilworth.
In his used Rambler, he drove his black comrades

to the mill when they shared turns.
His millhunk buddies ribbed him:

a jitney for spades. My father,
Thank God, was pensioned before steel quit Pittsburgh.

The payments of his first new car tick against him.
Last night, parking the Regal, he was stuck up.

"Three black bastards," he tells me
over the phone. *Don't make a sound,*

they said. *We'll blow your head off.*
This morning he left my mother's side,

tipped gently down the stairs, past the crucifix,
put an eye out for weather and started the coffee.

Then his silence for which he alone
has all these years so early risen to claim.

Outside is dark—ice, night
yet embedded in it, like steel.

The refuse truck grinds up the street.
Bandannaed garbage men march out of the white

feudal dawn into our backyard.
Rock salt burns a path for them.

Trash drums boom as they are hoisted.
The sun strikes itself on the frozen horizon.

1961

The house on Bigelow my father painted
for extra bread when yet again on strike
has not been painted since.
Constant boulevard traffic has turned its white

the color of exhaust. In '61,
my dad was 46—young. My mother,
sick of Union Wildcats at midnight, tried
coaxing him into leaving the mill for good.

A seamstress, she worked six nights till nine
on men's pants in Sears and Roebuck's tailor shop.
Each evening, my sister and I accompanied
my father to pick her up. If he was worried,

we never knew. Those nights: long,
coated in that dusky hour with solemnity,
as though everything had been turned down—
like praise: voices issuing from porches

where families listened to the Pirates on the radio,
my father conversing in Italian with them,
light stealing through streets and alleys,
around the houses. East Liberty:

sixteen years after VJ day, before the riots,
before Urban Renewal bombed it into a wasteland.
My father stopped and played a number
with a bookie outside Fox's Grille.

Stores up and down Highland Avenue
emptied, 9 straight up on the seminary clock,
pigeons peeling from the bell-tower
as the hour struck and people rushed the avenue.

Marie and I searched the crowds for my mother.
Smart-mouthed, with a walk that scared up everything
in her wake, we never spied her first.
She sprung out of nowhere, lipstick and silver

clip-on earrings like Roman battle shields.
"Give me a puff," she'd whisper,
putting her arms around my sister and me
as my father smiled and fitted his cigarette to her lips.

Then we'd get lemon ice at Moio's
and stroll home in the safety of our imagined
lives, across the last of the shoulder-high sun
shimmering in the steel of Hoeveler Street Bridge.

There was a house they wanted to buy.
They had rented all their lives.
There would never be a better time.
Was there tenderness those nights between my mother

and father? I fastened my eyes to earth,
sure that by sheer desire I'd discover something
that would end up mattering very much.
Later in my bed, listening to what sounded

like my parents telling secrets a floor below,
I was powerless against the dark washing me away.
Marie was smart enough to know what was going on,
but she kept to herself. Eventually

the Union settled and there was a new contract.
My father went back to climbing cranes.
at the Edgar Thomson Works in Braddock.
I can never drive down Bigelow Boulevard

without remembering that summer, 1961,
the $300 for which my father hung August-long
four stories over the Byzantine spires
of Polish Hill's Croatian temples.

All I could do when he was that high
was hold the ladder as paint rained on me.
When he ran out of rungs, he tied his brush
to a broom and painted like that

for three days until he finished—
so exhausted and blinded by paint
he couldn't make it back down,
and had to be helped inside

through a third floor window
by other strikers gathered to watch.
When my mother heard about it, she hissed:
"Dear God. You nearly killed yourself."

Marie threw herself upon him and cried.
He merely smiled.
He knew there was nothing
about him remarkable.

MAYDAY

From my bedroom window I can spit
on Vito and Mary's bed next door.
We slept that close.

But the freak eye of the May 1st blizzard
fixed on their house, crushing
Vito in his new Ford's plush.

Renegade snow beats down, turning back
the green that so stealthily tamed April.
Now the whole year is stunted.

Vito's Romas hang in their trusses;
azaleas buried to the red bud, withered.
Mary's floor is studded with china.

I told that son-of-a-bitch to stay home.
She sweeps her trousseau from the hutch,
stubbing out Camels on her thighs.

The pearl crown sits on its satin pillow
awaiting the coronation. The Madonna
smiles, the serpent wrapped around her

porcelain foot, impaled heart flaming
on the blue bodice. Each time Mary
lifts her handkerchief, glass crackles.

In the alley, a couple hobos lean
over a salamander. Vito used
to chase them off with a tire iron.

Kids sled into the Hollow's
white cup. Beneath them,
the earth curves.

WILD BILL AND DELILAH

Aunt Jay's husband, Wild Bill,
naked, save for his powder-blue boxer's,
watched the Pirates play on TV,
VO and water in one hand,

in the other an ice cream parfait,
his bashed pug mug
parched around a Lucky, false
sweet tooth racked in its partial plate.

Butts curled in the ashtray.
Rubbing the hair wiring out of his shrapneled paps,
he made smoke come out of his ears—
a trick at which I was unable to laugh.

He took me for bookish; I was petrified
of his black German Shepherd, Delilah,
lounging at his toenails, eating a baseball,
glowering, in her stunning jet habit.

He let her shit in my grandmother's next-door
yard and feed from the table.
Sitting perfectly still, not moving
my eyes from the game, the well

in me filled until, rather than flinch,
I began to pee. When my uncle noticed
my crotch darken, he laughed—a raw
phlegmy saw like *ack ack.*

When I sprang for the bathroom,
the dog struck—"just playing,"
my uncle lied, "he went for her ball."
I wore all summer the patch

over my bushwhacked eye, relearning
to see. No ballplaying,
but reading Stevenson, dreaming
in Braille of incubi with tetanus

needles. My grandmother declared
Wild Bill an *animale* when he punched the party
wall cleaving their kitchens.
The dog stayed.

I got older and drifted away.
When Aunt Jay died, I saw my uncle
at the funeral home, probably fifteen years
since we'd spoken. Because of my spectacles,

he smiled, called me *professor*—a joke,
his way of saying everything was okay.
Harmless, he cried; he prayed.
Old, with his wife gone,

he was finally exiled.
Sometimes I'd pass him, broken-
down, shy, murmuring, in Highland Park,
walking Delilah, by then enfeebled too,

her coat flecked gray, hindquarters arthritic.
He had to help her up steps and inclines.
Nights they went to Mount Carmel
and sat by the grave. I never spoke,

not knowing what to say.
The dog, with my blind unforgiving
ancestral blood in her maw,
still held vendetta's sway.

AUNT NINA IN MIDAIR

Aunt Nina, in hot pink sweats,
meets us at the door, holding
out her casted wrists, cracked
from her most recent fall.

Parkinson's has strung her like a puppet,
spooking to staggers her smile
and gander. At her beck,
jamming the sill, is her black nurse,

Gloria, who disappears
once her charge is commended to us.
We shuffle Aunt Nina to the couch
and sit at her feet the way we used to

as kids, innocent of *the souls*
of the faithfully departed, when she'd shake
out the fable of the child-eating Hollow
Bridge monster, Spacaluccio,

that sent us tearing to hide in her fur coats.
She'd laugh and spray us with atomized Emeraude.
She had the sunken cheeks, ascetic mien,
the blue mane of a Grimms' queen.

Our children are indifferent.
Lost in their own narratives,
they color and read, their memories
rearranging the texts of our lives.

Their maiden great-aunt pets them,
murmurs benediction, passing
over them the wand of fiction
that all will be well if we

thank God, even for malediction.
She looks herself a child, tiny,
lower lip pouting, arrowroot skin,
hair fretted from her forehead

with rhinestone barrettes.
On the wall above her head is the signed
gravure of John the XXIII.
Fat and aquiline in his satin skullcap,

his spavined script tracks ex-cathedrally
over the graying paper.
I've heard all my life Aunt Nina
should have married—instead of this.

I wander to her high-storey windows,
beneath which slinks the Hill District,
still taboo from the King war.
A statue of Saint Benedict the Moor

black-lords over the spate of barred stores
hawking the season in glyphic Yiddish.
Miles down the river, pale fire leaps
from the open hearth. A bridge seems

through the distorting flame
to slowly sink into the water.
For one vertiginous instant,
I know what it's like to be alone

in midair—and I can't bear it.
Yet there's music coming
from my aunt's bedroom;
and, when I enter it, I find Gloria,

oblivious to my presence, playing
an adagio—from what I couldn't say—
on a little keyboard one gives
a child for Christmas.

Suicide: Running Across the Meadow Street Bridge, Thanksgiving Day, 1993

The kid who took the bridge in '76,
the year I left home for the Bible Belt,

didn't die right away. A defaced plaque
remembering him lists on the light pole

in the middle of the deck. A junky
stiffed in a rat coat sits propped against it,

a smile stuffed into his nod. He doesn't flinch
as I jog over his bare ashen feet.

I've been warned again and again by those
who love me best: *Don't cross on foot.*

It's suicide. Crips, Bloods. Drive by's.
Parishioners with pistols playing chicken

on the parapets. Why I've come
is not clear to me. For the habit,

narcissism, perhaps, to be exorcised
of the old neighborhood that bars my entry

into a new trope. I'm sick of recounting
this past. Yet I still need to see

Lenora Street one last time,
my dead Godparents on their stoop notched

six feet below the sidewalk, waving
to me as I pose in my Little League flannels

for the Bell and Howell, a red roll
of caps set off like gunfire by a tiny

black boy with a brick in the middle
of Larimer Field. I sat through it—

we all did—the derogations, burned
into crude walled epistles or simply

mouthed like oblations. On my taboo run
I would if I could gallop the Christ over

this abyss for surely he would shimmer
long enough before shot to raise

those old Blacks and Italians grizzling
in their cerements and ask them how

of his liturgy they made this dying place.
What did the falling boy—

his name is silence—see below
in the Hollow mirror of concrete?

There's not much down there now:
a crysylic swamp hatching crossbred

catechists from its buckling aggregate.
His face is worn by his black double

who suddenly appears walking toward me,
an angel with the reaper's telltale gang hood.

He keeps his eyes on the bridge floor,
one hand secreted in his initiation blouse,

in the other a pair of black high-top All-Stars
he fits to the junky's naked feet.

Then he turns to me. "Fuck you,
Brother," he shouts. The streetlight whirs on,

spotting him for a second before he jumps.
I sprint to the rail and look over.

Nothing but the empty black cowl
floating over the few frighted cars chugging

up the Hollow Boulevard.
The freshly shod junky, in his miasma,

sighs and clicks open his eyes. In those tunnels
gleam twin versions of my white face peeking

out of the bridge dusk, my mouth agape,
swallowing the final round vowel of vertigo—

not a word, not even a syllable,
just the intake of breath, the sough before

an oath, the contagion of ancestry cursing
us to leave no message, no note, no nothing.

Rooted at this ledge where black and white
at Heaven's edge roil in a looted grail,

the weird trumpet of a ride roaring by wakes me.
I see within it brandished in the hands

of children fire. Then the conjured procession
convenes as the alleys and dead-ends spit

their ghosts. Beatified by fight and silence,
they wield rakes and shovels, spatulas, forks,

tomato stakes. Shed of pigment, they are the scorched
shades of mortification, enduring beyond the grave

for a last strike at their neighbor. And I,
their apostate son, am one of them, clinging

to the junky as the bridge in the clamor
of their warfare collapses.

Saint Marie Street

Sun sweeps the room. Whiskey
boils. The black-clad *comadres*
troop toward Our Lady's in confessional darkness

—across Meadow Street Bridge,
its rails now fenced
since summer's first suicide.

My father and Godfather stare
through the screen door
at this sorrowful procession—

as if reckoning absolution. They pour
shots and beers and tell a joke—
the kind, twenty years ago,

I was too young to laugh at—
about a guy who had to drink a fifth
of Black Velvet before confessing.

My laughter has a breaking to it—
remembering Father Dom cussing me out
after my first confession. Across the street,

little boys play hardball. Their bats
carom off the schoolyard's red cobblestones—
the refrain of my life.

I was on the same team as the kid who jumped—
hands that seemed to never touch the ball.
At eighteen he still collected baseball cards,

cocked his head like Clemente when he hit.
The whole street tried pinning it to something.
Noon church bells boom *The Angelus*.

Players fall to their knees—*an indulgence*
of ten years off Purgatory—doff
their black and gold Pirates caps

as the ball floats off. Even the hoods
on Chookie's corner cross themselves—
a nervous habit on Saint Marie

where Friday scorns flesh
and bookies make novenas.
Like punch-drunk fighters,

my fathers cover their faces.
Suddenly terrified at my lack of belief,
I turn in time to see the ball clear the fence

like a hightailing soul.
Even these two faithful sons of exile,
drinking without ever getting drunk,

holy pictures stuck to the walls around them—
whatever they know, they cannot utter:
The most you can hope for

is to hit a number
and die in your sleep,
forgiven.

LABORING

*Wherefore we labour, that, whether
present or absent, we may be accepted
of Him.*

— II Corinthians 5:9

(For Mark)

Our last job together was Fox Chapel—
an antique brick, black mortar, three
story mansion with six gables
chanceled into the tree-high eaves.

We had come to loathe heights,
dreaming each night of the scaffold,
the gantry with its rusty bucks
up to the warped gangplank

we tight-roped with hods, mortar
water washing black our naked backs.
Up there you could see, far-off,
the Allegheny—a river in the sky.

But directly below was an embattled
earth, shimmying in its litter of brazen
to the sway of the two-by-six upon
which I had turned stone, hod shouldered.

As though secreted even from themselves,
a sparge of brick men gazed up at me.
Empty mortar bags blew about their work boots.
They said nothing. In their faces was awe,

as if they wanted me to fall and couldn't
quite believe it themselves. Not that
they hated me, but because it would be a bad thing
that had happened to someone else.

They were already making of this a story
to tell their wives and children—
how random, Thank God, had spared them.
This was *their* lives—

not some college kid's working just the summer.
They wouldn't even remember my name.
I realized looking at them that I was
somehow theirs to scapegoat, that

through all their years of hod and scaffold,
they had conjured me to plummet,
that there was only one way to repay them
in their witness of the shattered work place.

I hung on the hod pole slatted at my neck.
Then among them your face shone,
eyes like blue coals meeting mine.
This was the dream we in our separate

cauls had nightly exchanged:
one of us stranded against a river of sky,
cradling a hundred pounds of deadweight.
Always just one of us, but which was never

obvious, nor was it that day
when I was ready to fall rather than risk
the disgrace of living; and you called,
Throw it down, and I did, watching

the top-heavy wedge-head whump into the site,
splashing black the weary masons,
now relieved and smiling and waiting
for me to crawl back down to earth.

FROM THE PHOTOGRAPH OF THE CHURCH STEPS: SEPTEMBER 3, 1947

My mother on her wedding day
clutches a gardenia bouquet.
The heady flowers have her ill,
but she refuses to complain.

It's her jaw, however, set to one side,
the left eye slightly closed,
that give her away.
She's wise-cracking out of the corner

of her mouth to the groom,
my father, who has her other hand
locked in his. He smiles the way
he smiles when busy understanding perfectly

there's no such thing as perfection.
Beautiful Isabelle, the Maid of Honor,
holds my mother's train above Meadow Street.
Next to her stands my mother's mother,

wearing a hat with flowers.
It is canon that women in church
cover their heads, and all of them
favor flowery wide-brims afloat

above their long hair. Dreadfully handsome,
the best man is Silvio Vento.
His bowtie is three clicks off keel,
one hand inside his tuxedo.

My mother despises him: "an operator,
a *gavone*." Man of great charm,
he will show up out of nowhere
twenty-one years later on the day

of my sister's graduation and, because
my dad is pulling shifts at the mill,
drive her to the Baccalaureate Mass;
then disappear again to his hideout in Florida.

Filling the church steps
trailing the newly wedded
are the families, mingling
in a hail of rice—

newsreel faces, unrecognizable
in the faded iconography of this forty-
five year old snapshot. Like Brueghel,
it becomes dizzying, too much.

I know so little. Where
is the dress? The boutonniere?
There are hardly any pictures.
My parents' modesty is unusual.

But in the arrangement of things, something
is already out of control. In the far left
of the photograph is a man, his back
to the camera. He rushes madly

back into Our Lady's. At the curb
hulks the honeymoon sedan,
in sun silvered like a mirror.
The windshield is halved by a blade-length

of chrome. Caught in the glass,
by some quirk of reflection, are the hands
of the bride and groom clasped in their bargain:
Good luck. Long life.

And I see now, only
now, for the first time, in the image
of the image of their interlocking hands
that knowing the future will not help them,

that my father is holding a cigarette
burnt down to his knuckles,
that he and my mother
are about to catch fire.

JOSEPH BATHANTI was born and raised in Pittsburgh, Pennsylvania. He is the author of six books of poetry: *Restoring Sacred Art*, winner of the 2010 Roanoke Chowan Award; *Land of Amnesia*, *Communion Partners*, *Anson County*; *The Feast of All Saints*; and *This Metal*, nominated for The National Book Award after it was first published by St. Andrews College Press in 1996. His books of fiction are *East Liberty*, *Coventry*, and *The High Heart*. He is also the author of *They Changed the State: The Legacy of North Carolina's Visiting Artists, 1971-1995*, a volume of nonfiction. He is Professor of Creative Writing at Appalachian State University in Boone, North Carolina.

CPSIA information can be obtained at www.ICGtesting.com
Printed in the USA
BVOW070100210512

290606BV00002B/10/P